Revive and Thrive

Revive and Thrive

Susan Mohan

Contents

First Printing, 2024

1

Understanding Your Current Situation

ASSESSING YOUR CHANNEL'S PERFORMANCE

Assessing your channel's performance is crucial for understanding how well your content resonates with your audience and what adjustments may be necessary to drive growth. Start by diving into YouTube Analytics, where metrics such as watch time, audience retention, and click-through rates provide valuable insights. These statistics reveal not only how many viewers are engaging with your content but also which videos are performing best. Identify patterns in viewer behavior, such as which types of videos lead to higher retention rates or generate more likes and comments. This data serves as a foundation for informed decision-making regarding your content strategy.

Audience engagement is another key aspect of performance assessment. Look beyond just views and subscriptions; examine how viewers interact with your videos. High engagement rates, reflected in likes, comments, and shares, indicate that your content is resonating with your audience. Consider conducting polls or soliciting feedback through comments to gain direct insights into what your audience enjoys or wants to see more of. Engaging with your audience not only fosters a sense of community but also provides qualitative data that can guide your content creation efforts.

Video SEO optimization is critical for enhancing your channel's discoverability. Assess how well your existing videos are optimized for search engines by examining keyword usage in titles, descriptions, and tags. Tools like Google Trends or keyword research tools can help identify popular search terms within your niche. By aligning your content with these terms, you can improve your chances of ranking higher in search results and attracting new viewers. Regularly reviewing and updating your video metadata based on performance data can lead to improved visibility over time.

Branding and channel aesthetics play a significant role in performance assessment as well. Take a critical look at your channel's overall presentation, including thumbnails, banners, and video intros. Cohesive branding helps create a memorable identity that can attract and retain subscribers. Analyze your channel's visual elements against competitors within your niche to identify areas for improvement. Creating visually appealing and on-brand thumbnails, for example, can significantly increase your click-through rates and encourage viewers to explore your content further.

Lastly, collaboration and networking strategies can enhance your channel's performance. Reach out to fellow creators within your niche for potential partnerships that can introduce your content to new audiences. Monitor the performance of collaborative videos to gauge their impact on your channel's growth. Additionally, leveraging social media platforms for promotion can expand your reach and drive traffic to your YouTube channel. Assess the effectiveness of your social media efforts by tracking referral traffic and engagement metrics to ensure that you are maximizing your promotional strategies. By continuously evaluating these aspects, you can create a dynamic approach to reviving and thriving on your YouTube channel.

IDENTIFYING REASONS FOR DECLINE

Identifying the reasons for decline in a YouTube channel is a crucial first step toward revitalization. Numerous factors can contribute to a drop in views, subscriber counts, or overall engagement. One of the most common issues is content stagnation. When creators fail to evolve their content or adapt to changing audience preferences, they risk losing relevance. This can happen if the content becomes repetitive, lacks innovation, or fails to capitalize on current trends. Therefore, evaluating the content strategy is essential to pinpoint what might be causing viewers to disengage.

Another significant factor can be audience engagement. Channels that do not actively interact with their viewers often find it challenging to maintain a loyal following. This lack of engagement can manifest through infrequent responses to comments, insufficient efforts to incorporate viewer feedback, or failure to create a community around the channel. Analyzing audience interaction metrics can reveal whether viewers feel valued and connected. If engagement is lacking, it may be time to implement new strategies, such as hosting Q&A sessions, creating polls, or involving viewers in content creation decisions.

Video SEO optimization is another area where channels often fall short. As the YouTube algorithm evolves, so do the best practices for optimizing video content to reach a broader audience. If a channel is not utilizing effective keywords, tags, and descriptions, it may be missing out on organic traffic. Conducting a thorough audit of existing videos and their performance can help identify gaps in optimization. Tools such as keyword research and competitor analysis can provide insights into the best strategies to improve visibility and attract new subscribers.

Branding and channel aesthetics also play a crucial role in a channel's success. A channel that lacks a cohesive brand identity or appealing visuals may struggle to attract and retain viewers. This includes everything from the channel banner and logo to video thumbnails and overall presentation style. An analysis of branding elements can reveal whether they align with the target audience's expectations and interests. Revamping these aspects can significantly enhance the channel's appeal and make it more memorable to potential viewers.

Lastly, collaboration and networking strategies should not be overlooked when identifying reasons for decline. Channels that operate in isolation may miss out on opportunities to reach new audiences through partnerships with other creators. Engaging in collaborations can provide fresh content ideas and introduce your channel to a wider demographic. Additionally, leveraging social media for promotion can amplify reach beyond the platform itself. By assessing current networking efforts and incorporating new collaboration strategies, creators can reignite interest in their channels and foster a more expansive community.

SETTING REVITALIZATION GOALS

Setting revitalization goals is a crucial first step in rejuvenating your YouTube channel. Establishing clear, measurable objectives helps provide direction and purpose to your efforts. Begin by evaluating your channel's current state and identifying specific areas that require improvement. Are you struggling with audience engagement, or is your content not reaching the intended demographic? By pinpointing these issues, you can formulate targeted goals that address your channel's unique challenges. Consider using the SMART criteria—Specific, Measurable, Achievable, Relevant, and Time-bound—to ensure your goals are well-structured and attainable.

For many creators, revitalization goals may focus on enhancing content strategy. This can include diversifying video formats, experimenting with different styles, or integrating trending topics relevant to your niche. Analyze successful channels similar to yours and identify what makes their content engaging. Set goals for the types of videos you want to produce and how often you plan to release them. For instance, aim to introduce a new video series within the next month or increase your upload frequency from bi-weekly to weekly. This not only keeps your audience engaged but also signals to the algorithm that your channel is active.

Audience engagement techniques should also be a priority when setting your revitalization goals. Cultivating a loyal community is essential for long-term success. Consider setting specific targets for audience interaction, such as increasing comments, likes, or shares on your videos. You might aim for a 20% increase in comments over the next quarter by implementing strategies like asking questions in your videos or hosting live Q&A sessions. Additionally, fostering connections through social media platforms can amplify your reach and encourage audience participation, leading to more dynamic engagement.

Another critical aspect of revitalization goals is video SEO optimization. As search algorithms become increasingly sophisticated, it's vital to ensure your content is easily discoverable. Set measurable goals for improving your video titles, descriptions, and tags to better align with search trends in your niche. For instance, you could aim to increase your average video ranking on search results by implementing SEO strategies over the next six months. Regularly analyzing your analytics can provide insights into which keywords are driving traffic and help you adapt your strategy accordingly.

Finally, consider establishing goals for collaboration and networking strategies. Collaborating with other creators can introduce your channel to new audiences and provide fresh content ideas. Set specific targets for how many collaborations you want to pursue within a certain timeframe. Networking can also extend to leveraging social media for promotion; aim to increase your presence on platforms like Instagram or Twitter by setting goals for follower growth or engagement rates. By integrating these elements into your revitalization plan, you'll create a comprehensive strategy that not only breathes new life into your channel but also fosters sustainable growth and improvement.

2

Reviving a Dead YouTube Channel

ANALYZING CONTENT GAPS

Analyzing content gaps is a crucial step in revitalizing a YouTube channel that may have lost its momentum. Content gaps refer to the areas where your existing videos fall short in meeting audience needs or where there is a lack of relevant content altogether. Identifying these gaps requires a thorough understanding of your niche, audience preferences, and competitor offerings. By evaluating these elements, you can pinpoint topics that resonate with viewers, ensuring that your new content is both engaging and valuable.

To effectively analyze content gaps, start by conducting a comprehensive review of your current video library. Look for patterns in viewer engagement metrics such as watch time, likes, comments, and shares. Identify videos that performed poorly and try to discern common themes or topics that may have contributed to their lack of success. This data-driven approach will help you understand what your audience craves and what types of content they may be bypassing. Additionally, leveraging YouTube Analytics can reveal search terms that led viewers to your channel, highlighting areas where you can expand or improve your offerings.

Next, evaluate your competitors within the same niche. Analyze their content strategies to see what topics they are covering and how they are engaging their audiences. Tools like VidIQ or TubeBuddy can provide valuable insights into the performance of competing channels, revealing their most successful videos and the gaps in their content as well. This competitive analysis can serve as a benchmark for your own content strategy, allowing you to identify underserved topics or unique angles that can set your channel apart from the rest.

Audience feedback is another critical component in identifying content gaps. Actively engage with your viewers through comments, polls, and social media to gain insights into what they want to see next. Encourage your audience to share their thoughts on your existing content and what topics they feel are missing. This direct line of communication fosters a sense of community and allows you to create content that is tailored to their interests, ultimately improving engagement and viewer loyalty.

Finally, once you have identified content gaps, it is essential to develop a strategic plan to address them. Create a content calendar that incorporates these new ideas, ensuring a balanced mix of topics that appeal to both existing subscribers and potential new viewers. Consider how each piece of content can be optimized for SEO, enhancing visibility and discoverability. Consistency in posting, combined with a clear focus on filling these gaps, will help breathe new life into your channel and set the stage for sustained growth and engagement.

REBRANDING YOUR CHANNEL

Rebranding your channel is a critical step for any YouTuber or streamer looking to breathe new life into their content and attract a fresh audience. This process involves revisiting the core elements of your channel, including its name, logo, visual identity, and overall messaging. A successful rebrand should resonate with both existing and prospective viewers, ensuring that the changes reflect your channel's evolution while remaining aligned with your niche. Begin by conducting a thorough analysis of your channel's current performance and audience demographics to identify areas needing improvement or re-alignment.

As you initiate the rebranding process, it is essential to establish a coherent visual identity that captures your channel's essence. This includes designing a new logo, banner, and thumbnail style that are not only visually appealing but also convey the theme and tone of your content. Consistency in your visual branding across all platforms can enhance recognition and loyalty among your audience. Consider seeking feedback from your viewers or conducting surveys to gauge their preferences, which can provide valuable insights into what elements resonate with them the most.

Beyond the visuals, your channel's name plays a pivotal role in its rebranding. A well-chosen name can effectively communicate your niche and content focus while being memorable and easy to search. If your current name no longer reflects your content or has become stale, consider brainstorming alternatives that capture the essence of what you aim to provide. However, ensure that your new name is easy to spell and pronounce, as this will encourage word-of-mouth recommendations and ease of discovery in search.

Engaging your audience during the rebranding process is crucial. Transparency about the changes you are implementing can foster a sense of community and inclusivity. Use social media platforms and community posts to communicate your rebrand, sharing your vision and inviting viewer feedback. Additionally, consider creating a special video announcement that outlines the changes, allowing viewers to understand the reasoning behind your rebranding efforts and encouraging them to embark on this new journey with you.

Finally, once your rebranding is complete, focus on promoting your revitalized channel through various strategies. Leverage social media to create buzz around your new identity, using teaser content and visuals that highlight the changes. Collaborations with other creators can also broaden your reach and introduce your rebranded channel to new audiences. Monitor your analytics closely to track the performance of your rebranding efforts, as this data will guide future content strategies and help refine your approach to audience engagement. By embracing a thoughtful and strategic rebranding process, you can effectively revive your channel and set it on a path to sustainable growth and success.

DEVELOPING A FRESH CONTENT APPROACH

Developing a fresh content approach is essential for revitalizing a stagnant YouTube channel. Many creators find themselves stuck in repetitive content cycles, which can lead to disengagement from their audience. To breathe new life into your channel, it is crucial to assess your current content strategy and identify areas for innovation. Start by analyzing what has previously resonated with your viewers and what has not. This insight will guide you in crafting a content plan that not only captures attention but also encourages viewers to return for more.

One effective technique is to incorporate audience feedback into your content development process. Engage with your subscribers through polls, comments, and social media platforms to understand their interests and preferences. This interaction not only fosters community but also provides valuable insights into what types of videos they want to see. By aligning your content with audience desires, you can create a more personalized experience that enhances viewer loyalty and encourages organic sharing of your videos.

Another vital aspect of developing a fresh approach is diversifying your content formats. Experimenting with different styles, such as vlogs, tutorials, live streams, and interviews, can attract new viewers and retain existing ones. Consider incorporating trending topics or challenges relevant to your niche to capture wider attention. Additionally, leveraging various visual and audio elements, such as animations or sound effects, can elevate the production quality of your videos and make them more engaging. A well-rounded content strategy that includes diverse formats can keep your audience intrigued and eager for your next upload.

Branding and channel aesthetics also play a critical role in revamping your content approach. Review your channel's visual elements, such as logos, thumbnails, and banner art, to ensure they reflect your updated content strategy. A cohesive visual identity can enhance recognition and create a professional appearance that attracts subscribers. Furthermore, consider creating a unique intro and outro for your videos to establish a consistent tone and branding across your channel. These elements not only make your content more visually appealing but also help viewers associate your videos with your brand.

Lastly, promote your revitalized content through strategic collaboration and effective use of social media. Partnering with other creators in your niche can introduce your channel to new audiences and provide fresh perspectives on content creation. Additionally, utilize platforms like Instagram, Twitter, and TikTok to share snippets or teasers of your YouTube videos, driving traffic back to your channel. Regularly analyzing your performance metrics will help you understand which promotional strategies yield the best results, allowing you to adjust your approach accordingly. By implementing these tactics, you can create a vibrant content ecosystem that fosters growth, engagement, and sustainability for your YouTube channel.

3

Crafting a Content Strategy Revamp

DEFINING YOUR NICHE

Defining your niche is a crucial step in revitalizing a YouTube channel that may have lost its momentum. A niche provides a specific focus that helps you stand out in a crowded marketplace. It allows you to target a particular audience segment, making your content more relevant and engaging. To define your niche effectively, start by assessing your interests, expertise, and the potential gaps in the market. This deep self-reflection will guide you in identifying a niche that not only excites you but also has the potential for audience growth and engagement.

Once you have a list of potential niches, conduct thorough research to understand the current landscape. Analyze successful channels within your areas of interest to identify what works and what doesn't. Pay attention to their content strategies, audience interactions, and branding choices. This analysis will help you discern trends and viewer preferences, enabling you to carve out a unique space for your channel. Consider engaging with your current audience or conducting surveys to gain insights into what they would like to see more of, ensuring your niche aligns with their interests.

In defining your niche, it's essential to focus on differentiation. Ask yourself what unique perspective or expertise you can bring to the table. This could be a specific style, a combination of topics, or a unique presentation method. The more distinct your niche, the easier it will be to attract and retain an audience. Emphasizing your personality and storytelling ability can further enhance your niche appeal, allowing you to create a connection with viewers that fosters loyalty and engagement.

Once you've settled on your niche, it's time to align your content strategy with it. Develop a content calendar that includes a mix of video types, such as tutorials, vlogs, interviews, or reviews, all tailored to your niche. Consistency is key; regular uploads help build viewer expectations and keep your audience returning for more. Additionally, utilize video SEO optimization techniques, focusing on keywords that resonate with your niche to improve discoverability. This strategic approach not only enhances viewer engagement but also positions your channel for growth.

Finally, leverage social media to promote your niche content and build a community around it. Sharing snippets or teasers of your videos on platforms like Instagram, Twitter, or TikTok can drive traffic to your channel. Engage with your audience through comments, polls, and Q&A sessions to foster a sense of belonging and loyalty. Collaborating with other creators in your niche can also expand your reach, exposing your channel to new audiences. By defining your niche clearly and strategically, you set the foundation for a revived and thriving YouTube channel that resonates with viewers and meets their needs.

CREATING A CONTENT CALENDAR

Creating a content calendar is an essential step for YouTubers and streamers looking to breathe new life into their channels. A well-structured content calendar not only helps in planning and organizing video releases but also ensures that you maintain consistency, which is crucial for audience retention and growth. To create an effective calendar, begin by identifying your target audience and their preferences. Understanding what resonates with your viewers will guide the type of content you should produce, increasing engagement and fostering a loyal community.

Once you have a clear picture of your audience, outline the types of videos you plan to create over the upcoming weeks or months. This could include tutorials, vlogs, live streams, or collaborative projects. Incorporate a mix of content that aligns with your niche while also experimenting with new ideas. For example, consider seasonal themes, trending topics, or challenges that can attract new viewers. By diversifying your content, you not only keep your channel fresh but also tap into different audience segments, enhancing your overall reach.

Scheduling is another critical component of a content calendar. Decide on a realistic posting frequency that fits your lifestyle and production capabilities. This could range from weekly uploads to bi-weekly or even monthly releases. Consistency is key, as it sets expectations for your audience and helps in building anticipation around your content. Make sure to factor in time for video production, editing, and promotion, as well as any unforeseen delays that might arise. A well-planned schedule can alleviate stress and keep your workflow organized.

Incorporating analytics into your content calendar can significantly enhance your strategy. Track the performance of your videos to determine which types of content resonate most with your audience. Use this data to inform future planning, adjusting your calendar as necessary based on viewer engagement metrics. This iterative approach not only optimizes your content strategy but also allows for timely pivots if certain topics or formats are underperforming.

Finally, consider how social media can complement your content calendar. Use platforms like Instagram, Twitter, or TikTok to tease upcoming videos, engage with your audience, and drive traffic to your YouTube channel. Schedule social media posts to align with your video releases, creating a cohesive promotional strategy. This multi-platform approach not only increases visibility but also strengthens your branding efforts. By effectively utilizing a content calendar, you can navigate the complexities of content creation while revitalizing your YouTube channel and enhancing audience engagement.

BALANCING EVERGREEN AND TRENDY CONTENT

Balancing evergreen and trendy content is crucial for YouTubers and streamers looking to revive their channels. Evergreen content refers to videos that remain relevant over time, addressing topics that consistently interest viewers regardless of current trends. Examples include how-to guides, tutorials, and in-depth explorations of niche subjects. On the other hand, trendy content capitalizes on current events, viral challenges, or popular topics that can draw immediate attention but may lose relevance quickly. A successful channel leverages both types of content to create a robust strategy that appeals to a broad audience while maintaining viewer engagement over the long term.

To effectively integrate evergreen content into your channel, consider your niche and audience preferences. Identify topics that have sustained interest and can provide value over time. This could involve creating comprehensive guides that address common questions or challenges within your niche. By establishing a library of evergreen videos, you create a foundation that continuously attracts new viewers and provides opportunities for cross-promotion with your trendy content. Regularly revisiting and updating these evergreen pieces can also enhance their SEO potential, ensuring they remain discoverable through search engines.

Incorporating trendy content requires agility and a keen awareness of what's currently engaging viewers. This could mean reacting to the latest news in your niche, taking part in viral challenges, or producing commentary on trending topics. The key is to align these trends with your channel's identity and audience interests, ensuring that the trendy content feels authentic and relevant. Balancing this with your evergreen strategy allows you to capture immediate interest while still fostering long-term viewer loyalty. It's important to monitor trends closely through social media and analytics tools to identify opportunities that resonate with your audience.

The interplay between evergreen and trendy content not only enhances audience engagement but also aids in effective branding and channel aesthetics. Consistent branding helps viewers recognize your content, whether it's a timeless tutorial or a timely reaction video. Utilizing similar visual elements, thumbnails, and intro/outro styles can create a cohesive channel identity that encourages viewers to explore both your evergreen videos and trendy offerings. This consistency helps build trust with your audience, making them more likely to return for both types of content.

Lastly, collaboration and networking strategies can amplify your efforts in balancing evergreen and trendy content. Partnering with other creators allows you to tap into their audience while sharing diverse perspectives on both timeless and timely topics. This cross-pollination can introduce your channel to new viewers who appreciate both your foundational content and your take on current trends. Additionally, engaging with your audience through comments and social media can provide insights into what they want to see more of, guiding your content strategy and ensuring that you strike the right balance moving forward.

4

Audience Engagement Techniques

BUILDING A COMMUNITY

Building a community around your YouTube channel is crucial for long-term success and engagement. A thriving community not only enhances viewer loyalty but also fosters an environment where audience members feel valued and connected. To establish this sense of belonging, start by understanding your audience's preferences and interests. Engage with them through comments, polls, and community posts, creating a two-way dialogue that encourages interaction. This engagement cultivates an atmosphere where viewers feel they have a stake in your channel's growth and direction, ultimately enhancing their commitment to your content.

Consistency is key when building a community. Regularly scheduled uploads and updates create anticipation among your viewers, making them more likely to return to your channel. Develop a content calendar that outlines your posting schedule and stick to it as closely as possible. This not only helps with audience retention but also allows you to plan themed content or series that can further engage your viewers. When your audience knows when to expect new content, they are more likely to engage with it actively and share it within their networks, amplifying your reach.

Collaboration and networking with other creators can significantly enhance your community-building efforts. By partnering with fellow YouTubers and streamers, you can tap into their audiences, exposing your channel to new viewers who may share similar interests. Look for creators whose content aligns with yours, and explore ways to collaborate, such as joint videos, live streams, or shout-outs. These collaborations not only diversify your content but also introduce your channel to a broader audience, fostering an interconnected community of creators and viewers alike.

Leveraging social media platforms is another effective strategy for building your community. Use platforms like Instagram, Twitter, and Discord to connect with your audience outside of YouTube. Share behind-the-scenes content, updates, and engage in conversations to deepen your relationship with your followers. Social media also provides an opportunity to solicit feedback on your content, which can guide your future videos and strengthen viewer investment in your channel. By creating a multi-platform presence, you can cultivate a more vibrant and engaged community that extends beyond the confines of YouTube.

Finally, tracking analytics is essential for understanding community dynamics and growth.

Use YouTube's built-in analytics tools to monitor viewer engagement, demographics, and behavior patterns. This data can inform your content strategy and help you identify what resonates most with your audience. By adapting your content based on these insights, you can foster a community that feels heard and valued, leading to enhanced loyalty and participation. Building a community is an ongoing process that requires dedication, but the rewards of a committed and engaged audience are invaluable for the revival and long-term success of your YouTube channel.

UTILIZING POLLS AND FEEDBACK

Utilizing polls and feedback is a powerful strategy for content creators looking to engage their audience and breathe new life into their YouTube channels. Polls provide a direct line of communication with viewers, allowing creators to gauge preferences, gather opinions, and understand audience interests on a granular level. By integrating polls into videos or posting them in the community tab, creators can encourage participation and make viewers feel valued. This interaction not only fosters a sense of community but also informs content decisions, ensuring that future videos are aligned with what the audience truly wants to see.

Feedback, whether solicited through comments or received through direct messages, is equally essential for revitalizing a channel. Creators should actively encourage viewers to share their thoughts on past content, including what resonated with them and what could be improved. This practice not only helps in fine-tuning the content strategy but also enhances viewer loyalty as audiences appreciate being heard. By openly discussing feedback in videos or community posts, creators can demonstrate their commitment to improvement, which can lead to increased engagement and a more dedicated subscriber base.

Incorporating feedback and poll results into content planning can lead to innovative and niche-specific ideas that resonate with the audience. For instance, if a poll indicates a strong interest in tutorials or behind-the-scenes content, creators can develop videos that cater specifically to those requests. This not only helps in reviving stagnant channels but can also position creators as responsive and adaptive within their niche. By consistently analyzing what viewers want, creators can maintain a dynamic content strategy that evolves alongside audience preferences.

Moreover, utilizing polls can significantly enhance video SEO optimization. When creators ask viewers to choose topics for future videos, they can strategically select keywords and phrases that reflect audience interests. This approach not only helps in optimizing titles and descriptions but can also improve discoverability, as content that aligns with viewer expectations is more likely to be shared and recommended. By intertwining audience feedback with SEO practices, creators can create a symbiotic relationship where both content quality and visibility are enhanced.

Finally, leveraging social media platforms to promote polls and collect feedback expands the reach of these initiatives. By sharing polls on Instagram, Twitter, or Facebook, creators can attract a broader audience and drive traffic back to their YouTube channel. Engaging with followers on multiple platforms builds a cohesive brand identity and reinforces the creator's commitment to audience involvement. Ultimately, by utilizing polls and feedback effectively, YouTubers and streamers can not only revive their channels but also cultivate a thriving community that actively participates in the content creation process.

RESPONDING TO COMMENTS EFFECTIVELY

Responding to comments effectively is a critical skill for YouTubers and streamers looking to enhance their audience engagement and revive their channels. Comments provide a direct line of communication between creators and their viewers, making it essential to approach them thoughtfully. Engaging with your audience in the comment section can foster a sense of community, encourage viewer loyalty, and ultimately contribute to the growth of your channel. By establishing a strategy for responding to comments, you can create a welcoming atmosphere that invites interaction and feedback.

One effective approach to responding to comments is to prioritize the ones that require immediate attention, such as questions or constructive criticism. Addressing these comments promptly shows your audience that you value their input and are committed to their experience. Additionally, responding to positive comments can enhance viewer satisfaction and encourage others to engage with your content. Personalizing your responses helps viewers feel seen and appreciated, which can translate into a more dedicated following over time.

Incorporating humor or personality into your responses can also make the interaction more enjoyable and memorable. A light-hearted reply can turn a simple comment into a fun exchange that encourages further dialogue. However, it's essential to maintain a professional tone, particularly when addressing negative feedback. Acknowledging criticism gracefully and offering solutions can transform a potentially damaging comment into an opportunity for growth. This not only demonstrates your commitment to improvement but also showcases your ability to handle challenges maturely.

Utilizing comment response strategies can also enhance your video SEO optimization. By including relevant keywords or phrases from viewer comments in your responses, you can maximize the visibility of your content. This practice can help boost your video's ranking in searches and attract new viewers who are looking for specific information. Additionally, encouraging viewers to leave comments by asking questions or soliciting feedback in your videos can create a continuous loop of engagement that benefits your channel's overall performance.

Lastly, consider leveraging social media platforms to extend the conversation beyond YouTube. Sharing standout comments or engaging discussions on your social media can drive traffic back to your channel and encourage more viewers to participate. This cross-platform engagement can help revitalize a stagnant channel and attract new audiences who resonate with your content. By implementing these techniques, you can not only respond to comments effectively but also create a thriving community that supports your channel's growth and success.

5

Video SEO Optimization

KEYWORD RESEARCH TECHNIQUES

Keyword research is a fundamental aspect of optimizing your YouTube channel, particularly when seeking to revive a stagnant or underperforming channel. The process begins with understanding the language and terms that your target audience is using when searching for content. Utilizing tools like Google Trends, YouTube's autocomplete feature, and keyword research platforms such as Ahrefs or SEMrush can provide invaluable insights into popular search queries. By identifying keywords relevant to your niche, you can tailor your content to meet the demands of viewers seeking specific information or entertainment, ultimately driving traffic to your channel.

Once you have compiled a list of potential keywords, categorizing them based on search intent is essential. Keywords can generally be divided into three categories: informational, navigational, and transactional. Informational keywords are often questions or phrases that viewers are curious about, while navigational keywords relate to specific brands or channels. Transactional keywords indicate a viewer's intent to make a purchase or engage with a service. By aligning your video content with the appropriate keyword category, you can better meet viewer expectations and increase engagement through likes, shares, and comments.

In addition to identifying and categorizing keywords, analyzing competitors can provide further clarity on effective keyword usage. Observing how similar channels implement their keywords in titles, descriptions, and tags can offer insights into successful strategies. Tools like VidIQ or TubeBuddy can help you assess the performance of competitors' videos and highlight the keywords they rank for. This competitive analysis allows you to identify gaps in their content that you can exploit, giving your channel a unique edge while also ensuring that you are targeting the same audience.

Incorporating keywords into your content effectively is as crucial as identifying them. Videos should have a well-optimized title that features your primary keyword, as well as a detailed description that elaborates on the video content while seamlessly integrating secondary keywords. Tags also play a significant role in video SEO, helping YouTube's algorithm understand the context of your video. Additionally, consider creating engaging thumbnails and channel art that reflect your keywords and overall branding. This cohesive approach not only enhances discoverability but also reinforces your channel's identity, making it more appealing to potential subscribers.

Finally, ongoing keyword research is vital for maintaining relevance in a rapidly evolving digital landscape. Trends can shift quickly, and what works today may not resonate tomorrow. Regularly revisiting your keyword strategy allows you to adapt to new interests and viewer behavior patterns. Utilize YouTube Analytics to track performance metrics related to specific keywords and adjust your content accordingly. By staying proactive in your keyword research efforts, you can ensure that your content remains fresh and engaging, ultimately breathing new life into your revived YouTube channel.

CRAFTING EFFECTIVE TITLES AND DESCRIPTIONS

Crafting effective titles and descriptions is crucial for grabbing the attention of potential viewers and improving your channel's discoverability. Titles should be concise yet descriptive, incorporating relevant keywords that resonate with your target audience. A well-structured title not only informs viewers about the content of the video but also piques their interest. Strive for a balance between creativity and clarity; a catchy title can draw in viewers, while a clear title ensures they know what to expect. Experiment with different styles and formats, such as questions or lists, to see what resonates best with your audience.

Descriptions serve as an extension of your title, providing context and additional information about your video. They offer an opportunity to include more keywords that improve your video's searchability on YouTube. Aim to craft a succinct summary that outlines the main points of your video while encouraging viewers to watch. Including timestamps can enhance user experience, especially for longer videos, allowing viewers to navigate to the sections that interest them most. Additionally, consider incorporating calls to action in your descriptions, prompting viewers to like, comment, subscribe, or check out related content.

SEO optimization plays a significant role in how effectively your titles and descriptions perform. Researching trending keywords and phrases in your niche can inform your title and description strategy. Tools like Google Trends or YouTube's own search suggestions can provide insights into popular search terms. Integrating these keywords naturally into both the title and description can enhance your video's visibility. Remember, however, to avoid keyword stuffing, which can lead to penalties from search algorithms and deter viewers from engaging with your content.

Branding is another essential aspect to consider when crafting titles and descriptions. Your titles should reflect your channel's tone and personality, helping to establish a consistent brand identity. This consistency extends to your descriptions, where you can reinforce your brand voice through language and style. Consider including a brief introduction about your channel in your descriptions, enabling new viewers to understand who you are and what kind of content you produce. This branding helps create a connection with your audience and can encourage them to subscribe for future content.

Finally, regularly reviewing and updating your titles and descriptions can lead to improved performance over time. Analyze your video analytics to see which titles and descriptions yield the best engagement rates, and be willing to make adjustments. Experiment with A/B testing by changing titles or descriptions on older videos to see if you can boost their performance. Engaging with your audience through comments can also provide valuable feedback on your titles and descriptions, giving you insight into what resonates with them. Adapting your approach based on performance and audience feedback will ensure your titles and descriptions remain effective tools in your content strategy.

UTILIZING TAGS AND THUMBNAILS

Utilizing tags and thumbnails is essential for enhancing the visibility and appeal of your YouTube channel. Tags play a crucial role in helping the YouTube algorithm understand the context of your videos. By strategically selecting and utilizing relevant tags, you can improve your video's chances of appearing in search results and suggested videos. It's important to include a mix of broad and specific tags; broad tags capture a wider audience, while specific tags target niche viewers who are more likely to engage with your content. Researching popular tags in your niche can provide insight into what potential viewers are searching for, allowing you to tailor your tags accordingly.

Thumbnails serve as the first impression of your video and can significantly influence a viewer's decision to click. A custom thumbnail that is visually appealing and reflects the content of the video can increase click-through rates. To create effective thumbnails, consider using bold text, vibrant colors, and eye-catching imagery that conveys the essence of your video. Consistency in your thumbnail design helps establish your brand identity, making it easier for viewers to recognize your content amidst a sea of videos. Ensure that your thumbnails are optimized for various devices, as many users access YouTube on mobile phones or tablets.

Combining well-optimized tags with compelling thumbnails can enhance audience engagement. When viewers find your videos through search or recommendations, the synergy between your tags and thumbnails can lead to higher watch times and lower bounce rates. This, in turn, signals to YouTube that your content is valuable, potentially boosting your rankings in search results and suggested video feeds. It's essential to analyze the performance of your tags and thumbnails regularly, allowing you to make data-driven adjustments that can improve viewer retention and engagement over time.

In addition to attracting viewers, tags and thumbnails play a role in your overall branding strategy. Consistent use of visuals and terminology across your thumbnails and tags reinforces your channel's identity. This not only helps in establishing a recognizable brand but also builds trust with your audience, as they come to associate specific styles and themes with your channel. Engaging with your audience through comments and social media can provide insights into how they perceive your branding, allowing you to refine your approach further.

Lastly, utilizing tags and thumbnails effectively can enhance your collaboration and networking efforts. When collaborating with other creators, ensure that your tags and thumbnails align with the content of the partnership. This strategy can attract the collaborator's audience to your channel, facilitating growth and engagement. Additionally, leveraging social media to showcase your videos with attention-grabbing thumbnails can drive traffic back to your YouTube channel. By integrating tags and thumbnails into your comprehensive content strategy, you can breathe new life into your channel, making it more appealing and accessible to both new and existing viewers.

6

Branding and Channel Aesthetics

DESIGNING A COHESIVE VISUAL IDENTITY

Designing a cohesive visual identity is crucial for any YouTuber or streamer looking to revitalize their channel and engage their audience effectively. A strong visual identity not only makes your content easily recognizable but also communicates your brand's values, personality, and niche. When creating a visual identity, consider the essential components such as your logo, color scheme, typography, and overall aesthetic. These elements should work harmoniously together to create a unified look that reflects your channel's theme and resonates with your target audience.

Start by developing a logo that encapsulates your brand essence. This logo will serve as the cornerstone of your visual identity, appearing across all your content, including video thumbnails, social media profiles, and merchandise. A well-designed logo is simple yet memorable, allowing viewers to associate it with your content instantly. Take the time to brainstorm ideas, sketch concepts, and refine your design. Tools like Canva or Adobe Illustrator can aid in creating a professional-looking logo that aligns with your channel's vibe.

Next, choose a color palette that complements your logo and overall theme. Colors evoke emotions and can significantly influence how your audience perceives your brand. For instance, vibrant colors might convey excitement and energy, while softer tones could communicate a calm and inviting atmosphere. Consistency in color usage across your thumbnails, channel art, and social media posts will create a cohesive visual experience for your viewers. Use tools like Adobe Color or Coolors to explore color combinations that align with your channel's message.

Typography is another critical aspect of your visual identity. Selecting the right fonts enhances readability and reinforces your brand's personality. A combination of two or three complementary fonts can create a balanced and professional look. Use one font for headings, another for body text, and perhaps a third for accents or quotes. Be mindful of font styles that fit your niche; for example, a gaming channel might opt for bold, modern fonts, while a beauty channel might choose elegant, script fonts. Consistency in typography across all platforms will further solidify your brand identity.

Finally, ensure your visual identity translates well across various platforms and content types. From video intros and overlays to social media graphics and website banners, maintaining a cohesive aesthetic is key. This approach not only enhances brand recognition but also builds trust with your audience. Regularly review and update your visual elements as your channel evolves, ensuring they continue to reflect your growth and changes in content strategy. By investing time and effort into designing a cohesive visual identity, you position your channel for long-term success and engagement.

CREATING EYE-CATCHING THUMBNAILS

Creating eye-catching thumbnails is essential for attracting viewers and increasing engagement on your YouTube channel. Thumbnails serve as the first impression of your video, making them a critical element in your content strategy. A well-designed thumbnail can significantly improve click-through rates, drawing in viewers who might otherwise overlook your video. To craft effective thumbnails, consider incorporating bold colors, striking images, and clear text that conveys the essence of your video. By understanding your audience's preferences and visual trends, you can create thumbnails that resonate with viewers and encourage them to click.

One of the most important aspects of thumbnail creation is simplicity. A cluttered or overly complex thumbnail can confuse viewers, leading them to scroll past your video. Aim for a clean design that highlights the main subjects or themes of your content. Use high-resolution images that are relevant to the video topic and avoid using too many elements that can detract from the central message. Consistency in style across your thumbnails helps establish your brand identity, making it easier for viewers to recognize your content at a glance.

Incorporating text into your thumbnails can enhance their effectiveness, especially when it comes to conveying what your video is about. Use short, impactful phrases that capture the video's core message and evoke curiosity. Ensure that the font is legible even at smaller sizes, as many viewers will encounter your thumbnail on mobile devices. Utilizing contrasting colors for text and background can further improve readability and grab attention. Experimenting with different fonts, sizes, and placements can help you discover the most effective combinations for your audience.

Another vital aspect of thumbnail design is the use of branding elements. Including your logo or a consistent color scheme can help reinforce your brand identity and make your content easily recognizable. This is particularly important for channels focusing on reviving their presence, as a cohesive visual identity can help build trust and familiarity among viewers. Additionally, consider using a specific style or theme for your thumbnails that aligns with your niche, which can further engage your target audience and encourage them to explore more of your content.

Finally, it is important to test and analyze the performance of your thumbnails regularly. Utilize YouTube analytics to track which thumbnails generate the highest click-through rates and audience retention. This data can provide valuable insights into what resonates with your viewers, allowing you to refine your approach over time. Engaging with your audience through comments or social media can also yield feedback on your thumbnails. By continually evolving your thumbnail strategy based on performance metrics and audience preferences, you can enhance your video's visibility and boost your channel's overall success.

DEVELOPING A CONSISTENT TONE AND VOICE

Developing a consistent tone and voice is essential for any YouTuber or streamer looking to revive their channel and engage their audience effectively. A clear and distinct voice helps to create a recognizable brand, making it easier for viewers to connect with the content on a personal level. This connection is crucial, especially when trying to rekindle interest in a channel that may have fallen dormant. A well-defined tone resonates with the target audience, reflecting their preferences and expectations, which can significantly enhance viewer retention and loyalty.

To establish this consistency, creators should first identify the core values and themes that represent their content. This involves reflecting on what the channel stands for and the message it aims to convey. Whether it's humor, education, inspiration, or a mix of these, having a foundation allows creators to craft content that aligns with their identity. This foundation not only aids in scripting and delivery but also informs visual elements, ensuring that every aspect of the channel works in harmony to reinforce the desired tone.

Moreover, maintaining a consistent tone across different types of content is vital. For instance, a channel that typically features lighthearted commentary should avoid drastic shifts to overly serious topics without proper transition. This doesn't mean that content cannot evolve; rather, it should do so gradually, ensuring that the audience feels a sense of continuity. Audience expectations can be tightly linked to the established voice, and sudden changes can lead to confusion or disengagement, undermining the channel's revival efforts.

Engagement with the audience also plays a crucial role in refining tone and voice. Creators should actively seek feedback through comments, polls, and social media interactions to gauge how their audience perceives their content. This engagement not only fosters a community atmosphere but also provides insights into what resonates best with viewers. By understanding their audience's preferences, creators can fine-tune their voice to better align with viewer expectations, thus enhancing overall engagement and satisfaction.

Finally, consistency in tone and voice extends beyond individual videos to encompass the entire channel's branding and aesthetics. Elements such as thumbnails, channel trailers, and video descriptions should reflect the established voice, creating a cohesive experience for viewers. This uniformity helps in building brand recognition, making it easier for potential new subscribers to understand what to expect from the channel. As creators focus on reviving their channels, they should prioritize the development of a consistent tone and voice, as this is foundational to achieving sustainable growth and lasting audience engagement.

7

Collaboration and Networking Strategies

IDENTIFYING POTENTIAL COLLABORATORS

Identifying potential collaborators is essential for revitalizing a YouTube channel and enhancing its reach. Collaborations can introduce your content to new audiences, breathe fresh life into your video ideas, and help you learn from others in your niche. To effectively identify potential collaborators, start by analyzing creators who share a similar audience but do not directly compete with your channel. This ensures that both parties can benefit from the partnership without alienating their respective viewers. Look for creators who create content in complementary niches, as this can lead to innovative video ideas that appeal to both audiences.

Another effective strategy is to engage with creators whose work you genuinely admire. Follow them on social media, participate in their discussions, and comment on their videos. By establishing a rapport, you can create a foundation of trust and mutual respect, making it easier to approach them for collaboration. Pay attention to creators who actively engage with their audience, as this indicates a strong community that can be leveraged for your own channel's growth. Building genuine relationships in the YouTube community will not only help you identify potential collaborators but also enhance your own credibility.

When considering potential collaborators, evaluate their content quality and consistency.

Look for creators who maintain a professional level of production and have a reliable posting schedule. This will ensure that any collaboration reflects well on both parties involved. Analyze their engagement metrics, such as likes, comments, and shares, to gauge how well their audience responds to their content. A creator with high engagement is more likely to bring additional viewers and subscribers to your channel through a collaborative effort.

Utilizing social media platforms can also aid in identifying potential collaborators. Platforms like Instagram, Twitter, and TikTok are great for discovering creators who align with your brand and values. Join niche-specific groups or forums to find like-minded individuals who are also looking to collaborate. Sharing your ideas and being open to suggestions can lead to fruitful partnerships. Additionally, attending virtual or in-person events related to your niche can provide opportunities to meet potential collaborators face-to-face, fostering connections that may lead to successful collaborations in the future.

Finally, don't overlook the importance of diversity in your collaborations. Engaging with creators from different backgrounds, styles, and perspectives can enrich your content and attract a broader audience. Consider collaborating with creators who focus on various aspects of your niche, whether it's a different format, such as live streaming, tutorials, or challenges. This not only enhances your channel's appeal but also encourages innovation and creativity in your content strategy. By thoughtfully selecting collaborators, you can create dynamic content that stands out and resonates with a diverse audience, ultimately leading to a revived and thriving YouTube channel.

APPROACHING OTHER CREATORS

Approaching other creators is a crucial strategy for YouTubers and streamers looking to revive their channels and expand their reach. Collaboration can infuse new energy into your content while providing opportunities for audience growth. When considering how to approach fellow creators, it's important to first identify individuals whose content aligns with your niche and audience. This alignment ensures that both parties benefit from the collaboration, fostering a natural and engaging experience for viewers. Take the time to research their channels, understand their style, and analyze their audience demographics to find the best match.

Once you've pinpointed potential collaborators, crafting a personalized message is vital. Generic outreach can often lead to missed opportunities, as it fails to demonstrate genuine interest in the other creator's work. Highlight specific aspects of their content that you admire, and propose collaboration ideas that would be mutually beneficial. Whether it's a joint video, a shoutout, or a guest appearance, your proposal should reflect an understanding of their channel and how a partnership might enhance both your audiences. This personalized approach not only increases the likelihood of a positive response but also builds a foundation for a meaningful relationship.

In addition to direct collaboration, networking within creator communities can amplify your outreach efforts. Engage with other creators by participating in online forums, attending industry events, or joining social media groups focused on content creation. This engagement can lead to organic connections with other creators who share your passion and goals. Building relationships over time, rather than seeking immediate collaboration, can result in more fruitful partnerships down the line. Networking should be viewed as a long-term strategy, where mutual support and sharing of resources can lead to innovative content opportunities.

Another effective tactic is to leverage social media platforms to showcase your intent to collaborate. Creating posts that highlight your willingness to partner with others, such as sharing past collaborations or discussing potential projects, can attract creators who are looking for similar opportunities. Use relevant hashtags and tag creators you admire, which can initiate conversations and pique their interest. Engaging with their content by liking, commenting, and sharing can also help you become a familiar presence, making them more receptive to collaboration proposals.

Finally, it's essential to approach collaborations with a spirit of creativity and flexibility. Be open to different ideas and formats, as the best collaborations often emerge from brainstorming sessions where both creators contribute their unique perspectives. Establish clear communication regarding expectations, timelines, and goals to ensure a smooth collaboration process. By nurturing these partnerships, you can not only revive your channel but also create a supportive community of creators who inspire and uplift one another, ultimately leading to sustained growth and engagement.

CROSS-PROMOTION TECHNIQUES

Cross-promotion techniques are essential tools for YouTubers and streamers looking to revitalize their channels and engage a broader audience. These strategies allow creators to tap into existing audiences from other platforms or channels, fostering a sense of community and driving traffic back to their primary content. By collaborating with other creators, utilizing social media, and engaging with niche communities, you can create a dynamic ecosystem that supports your channel's growth.

One effective method of cross-promotion is collaboration with other YouTubers or streamers in your niche. By partnering on videos or live streams, you can introduce your content to their audience while providing value through joint discussions or challenges. This not only expands your reach but also enhances the viewing experience by combining different perspectives and styles. When selecting collaborators, consider those whose content complements yours; this ensures that the audience is likely to appreciate both creators' offerings.

Social media platforms serve as powerful venues for cross-promotion. Sharing snippets, behind-the-scenes content, or engaging posts related to your videos can attract attention and drive traffic to your channel. Each platform has its strengths; Instagram is ideal for visual content, Twitter for quick updates and conversations, and TikTok for short, engaging clips. By tailoring your promotional strategies to fit the unique characteristics of each platform, you can effectively capture the interest of potential viewers and encourage them to explore your YouTube channel.

Engaging with niche-specific communities can also significantly enhance your cross-promotion efforts. Participating in forums, Facebook groups, or Discord servers related to your content allows you to build relationships with like-minded individuals who may be interested in your videos. By contributing valuable insights or sharing your content in a non-intrusive way, you can establish yourself as a credible member of the community, making it more likely that they will check out your channel. Authentic engagement is key; focus on building relationships rather than merely promoting your work.

Finally, analyzing the effectiveness of your cross-promotion strategies is crucial for ongoing success. Utilize analytics tools to track referral traffic and viewer engagement resulting from your promotional efforts. This data can inform your future strategies, allowing you to identify which techniques yield the best results. By continually refining your approach based on performance metrics, you can ensure that your cross-promotion techniques evolve alongside your channel, maximizing your potential for growth and audience engagement.

8

Leveraging Social Media for Promotion

CHOOSING THE RIGHT PLATFORMS

Choosing the right platforms for promoting your YouTube channel is a critical step in revitalizing your online presence. While YouTube is the primary platform for video content, leveraging additional platforms can significantly enhance your reach and engagement. Consider where your target audience spends their time and what type of content they prefer. Popular social media platforms such as Instagram, TikTok, and Twitter can complement your YouTube efforts, allowing you to create a multi-channel strategy that drives viewers back to your main videos.

Each platform has its unique characteristics and audience demographics, so it is essential to tailor your content accordingly. For instance, Instagram is visually driven and works well for behind-the-scenes content, teasers, or engaging stories that pique interest in your YouTube videos. TikTok, with its short-form video content, offers a great opportunity to create quick, entertaining snippets that can go viral and direct traffic to your channel. Understanding the nuances of each platform will help you craft content that resonates with users and encourages them to engage with your YouTube channel.

Additionally, consistency across platforms is key to building a cohesive brand identity. Ensure that your branding elements, such as logos, colors, and messaging, are consistent across all platforms. This not only helps in establishing a recognizable brand but also creates a seamless experience for your audience as they interact with your content across different channels. A well-defined brand identity can significantly enhance audience trust and loyalty, making them more likely to engage with your videos and share them within their networks.

Engagement techniques also vary by platform, and it's crucial to leverage each platform's strengths to foster audience interaction. For example, utilizing polls and interactive stories on Instagram can encourage viewer participation and feedback, which can inform your content strategy on YouTube. Similarly, engaging with your audience through live streams on platforms like Twitch or Facebook can build a community around your channel, enhancing viewer loyalty and increasing the likelihood of regular viewership on your YouTube uploads.

Finally, don't underestimate the power of analytics in refining your platform choices. Each social media platform provides insights into audience behavior and content performance. Regularly monitoring these analytics allows you to adapt your strategy based on what works best in driving traffic to your YouTube channel. By analyzing which platforms bring in the most engagement and views, you can allocate your resources effectively, ensuring that your efforts yield the best possible results for your revitalized channel.

CREATING SHAREABLE CONTENT

Creating shareable content is crucial for revitalizing your YouTube channel and enhancing audience engagement. Shareable content typically resonates with viewers on an emotional level, prompting them to share it with their own networks. To achieve this, start by identifying your target audience's interests and pain points. Conduct surveys, analyze comments, and leverage social media insights to gather data about what your audience values most. By aligning your content with their preferences, you significantly increase the likelihood of shares and interactions.

Incorporating storytelling into your videos is an effective strategy for creating shareable content. People naturally gravitate towards narratives that evoke emotions, whether it be humor, inspiration, or nostalgia. Craft stories that reflect your personal experiences or that of your audience, tying them back to your niche. This connection not only makes your content more relatable but also encourages viewers to share their own stories in the comments, fostering a sense of community around your channel.

Visual appeal plays a pivotal role in shareability. Invest time in refining your video aesthetics, including thumbnails, graphics, and overall production quality. A captivating thumbnail can be the difference between a viewer clicking on your video or scrolling past it. Additionally, use eye-catching visuals and engaging editing techniques to maintain viewer interest throughout the video. High-quality visuals not only enhance the overall experience but also encourage viewers to share content that looks professional and polished.

Encouraging viewer interaction is vital for creating shareable content. Incorporate calls to action throughout your videos, inviting viewers to comment, like, and share. Pose questions that prompt discussions or create polls that engage your audience in decision-making processes related to your content. By fostering an interactive environment, you make your viewers feel valued, which can lead to increased sharing as they want their friends and family to join the conversation.

Finally, leverage social media platforms to amplify your shareable content. Once you have created videos that resonate with your audience, promote them across various social media channels. Tailor your promotional strategies to each platform, using relevant hashtags and engaging captions to optimize visibility. Collaborate with other creators in your niche to reach broader audiences and encourage cross-promotion. By actively promoting your content and engaging with viewers beyond YouTube, you create a multifaceted approach that can significantly enhance the shareability of your videos.

ENGAGING WITH FOLLOWERS ON SOCIAL MEDIA

Engaging with followers on social media is an essential strategy for YouTubers and streamers looking to breathe new life into their channels. In today's digital landscape, social media serves as a powerful tool to build relationships with your audience, enhance brand visibility, and drive traffic to your YouTube content. By actively maintaining a presence on platforms such as Instagram, Twitter, and Facebook, creators can foster a community that not only supports their work but also contributes to the channel's growth. This engagement is crucial for reviving a stagnant channel, as it encourages viewers to return and engages them in meaningful ways.

To effectively engage with followers, creators should prioritize authentic interactions. Responding to comments, sharing user-generated content, and asking for feedback on upcoming videos can create a dialogue that resonates with your audience. This two-way communication establishes a sense of belonging and loyalty among viewers, which is particularly important for reviving a dead channel. When followers feel valued and heard, they are more likely to share your content, recommend your channel to others, and participate actively in discussions, further enhancing your reach and visibility.

Incorporating engaging content formats is another effective way to connect with followers on social media. Live streams, Q&A sessions, polls, and behind-the-scenes glimpses into your creative process can capture the interest of your audience and encourage them to interact more. These formats not only humanize your brand but also provide an opportunity for viewers to engage with you in real-time, creating a memorable experience. This interaction can help to solidify your relationship with your audience, making them feel more invested in your channel's success.

Moreover, leveraging social media analytics can provide valuable insights into what resonates with your audience. By tracking engagement metrics such as likes, shares, and comments, creators can identify trends and preferences that inform their content strategy. This data-driven approach allows for the optimization of future posts and videos, ensuring that creators are meeting the needs and interests of their audience. Understanding which topics spark conversation or which formats garner the most engagement can guide creators in planning their content, ultimately leading to a more successful revival of their channel.

Lastly, collaboration and networking on social media can amplify your reach and enhance engagement. Partnering with other creators or influencers can introduce your channel to new audiences and provide fresh perspectives to your content. By engaging with their followers and encouraging cross-promotion, you can create a mutually beneficial relationship that fosters growth for both parties. Additionally, participating in relevant online communities can further expand your network, allowing you to connect with potential collaborators and engage with a wider audience, ultimately revitalizing your YouTube channel and nurturing a thriving online community.

9

Analytics and Performance Tracking

UNDERSTANDING YOUTUBE ANALYTICS

Understanding YouTube Analytics is crucial for any YouTuber or streamer looking to breathe new life into their channel. YouTube provides a wealth of data that can help creators understand their audience, track performance, and refine their content strategies. By delving into YouTube Analytics, creators can uncover insights about who is watching their videos, how they found them, and which content resonates most. This information is vital for making informed decisions that can lead to channel growth and improved viewer engagement.

One of the key metrics to focus on is watch time, which indicates how long viewers are watching your videos. This metric is particularly important because YouTube prioritizes videos with higher watch times in its algorithm, making them more likely to be recommended to new viewers. By analyzing watch time data, creators can identify which videos keep viewers engaged and which ones might benefit from re-editing or additional promotional efforts. Understanding audience retention graphs can also reveal specific points in videos where viewers drop off, providing opportunities to adjust content to maintain engagement.

Another essential component of YouTube Analytics is the traffic source report. This data helps creators understand where their views are coming from, whether through search results, suggested videos, or external sources. By identifying the most effective traffic sources, YouTubers can tailor their promotional strategies and optimize their video SEO. For instance, if a significant portion of views comes from search, focusing on keyword optimization in titles, descriptions, and tags becomes even more critical. Conversely, if suggested videos are driving traffic, creators may want to analyze their thumbnails and titles to improve click-through rates.

Audience demographics also play a significant role in shaping content strategy. YouTube Analytics provides insights into viewers' age, gender, and location, allowing creators to tailor their content to meet the preferences and interests of their specific audience. Understanding the demographics can help in crafting niche-specific content ideas that resonate more deeply with viewers. Moreover, this knowledge can inform collaboration and networking strategies, as creators can seek partnerships with others who share a similar audience or brand values, leading to mutually beneficial growth.

Finally, tracking performance over time is vital for long-term success on YouTube. Regularly reviewing analytics enables creators to spot trends and shifts in viewer behavior, allowing for timely adjustments to content and promotion strategies. Consistency in analyzing data ensures that creators remain agile and responsive to their audience's needs. Utilizing analytics not only enhances video performance but also aids in developing a cohesive branding strategy across the channel. By integrating insights from YouTube Analytics into their overall content approach, creators can effectively revive and thrive in the competitive landscape of YouTube.

KEY METRICS TO MONITOR

To effectively revive and thrive on YouTube, it is essential to monitor key metrics that provide insights into channel performance. One of the most critical metrics is watch time, which measures the total minutes viewers spend watching your videos. By tracking watch time, you can identify which content resonates with your audience and which does not. A focus on increasing watch time can lead to better ranking in YouTube's algorithm, ultimately resulting in greater visibility and potentially more subscribers. Assessing watch time alongside average view duration can help pinpoint specific areas for improvement in your content strategy.

Another vital metric is audience retention, which indicates the percentage of viewers who remain engaged throughout your video. A high audience retention rate suggests that your content is captivating and relevant to your viewers. To enhance this metric, consider experimenting with different formats, storytelling techniques, or hooks at the beginning of your videos. Analyzing where viewers drop off can provide valuable feedback on what aspects of your video may need refinement, aiding in the development of more engaging content moving forward.

Engagement metrics, such as likes, comments, and shares, also play a significant role in gauging your audience's connection to your channel. High levels of engagement not only reflect the quality of your content but also influence YouTube's algorithm in favor of promoting your videos. Encouraging viewers to interact through calls to action can foster a sense of community and loyalty among your audience. Additionally, responding to comments and fostering discussions can enhance viewer engagement, making your channel a more inviting space for both new and returning viewers.

Subscriber growth rate is another essential metric to monitor as it reflects how well your content is attracting and retaining viewers. A steady increase in subscribers indicates that your content is resonating with your target audience, while sudden spikes can signal the success of particular videos or strategies. It is important to analyze the correlation between your content and subscriber growth, as this can inform future content strategies. Implementing consistent branding and aesthetics can also enhance your channel's appeal, making it more likely for viewers to subscribe.

Finally, leveraging YouTube Analytics to track traffic sources and audience demographics can provide insights into how viewers discover your channel. Understanding whether your traffic comes from search, suggested videos, or external sources like social media can help you refine your promotional strategies. Additionally, demographic data can inform your content creation by highlighting the interests and preferences of your audience. By regularly monitoring these key metrics, you can make informed decisions that will lead to sustained growth and success for your revived YouTube channel.

USING DATA TO INFORM FUTURE CONTENT

Using data to inform future content is a critical strategy for YouTubers and streamers aiming to breathe new life into their channels. By analyzing performance metrics and audience behavior, creators can gain valuable insights that guide their content strategy. This data-driven approach allows them to identify what resonates with viewers, which can lead to higher engagement, improved video SEO, and ultimately, channel growth. Understanding the importance of data not only enhances content quality but also helps in building a loyal audience that feels seen and heard.

One of the most significant metrics to consider is audience retention. By examining how long viewers stay engaged with a video, creators can determine which segments hold their attention and which parts may cause them to drop off.

This information is essential for refining video structure and pacing. For instance, if viewers consistently leave during a specific segment, it might indicate that the content is either too slow or lacks interest. Adjusting these elements can lead to stronger viewer retention and increased likelihood of subscribers, thus revamping the overall content strategy.

Engagement metrics, such as likes, comments, and shares, provide further insight into what content types resonate most with the audience. Analyzing which videos generate the most interaction allows creators to replicate successful formats or topics. Additionally, diving into the comments can reveal viewer preferences and suggestions, creating an avenue for deeper audience engagement. Implementing feedback from the community can foster a sense of belonging among viewers, encouraging them to return and interact more consistently with the channel.

Video SEO optimization is another area where data plays a crucial role. By studying search terms and traffic sources, creators can identify effective keywords and trends that attract viewers. Utilizing tools like Google Trends and YouTube Analytics can help uncover niche-specific content ideas, ensuring that future videos align with what audiences are actively searching for. This not only boosts visibility but also positions the channel as a relevant and authoritative source within its niche, enhancing brand perception.

Lastly, consistency in content scheduling can be informed by data. Analyzing when viewers are most active on the platform allows creators to publish videos at optimal times, increasing the likelihood of immediate engagement. Additionally, tracking performance over time can help determine the best frequency for content delivery, whether it's weekly, bi-weekly, or monthly. By aligning production schedules with data insights, creators can maintain momentum and keep their channels vibrant and thriving. This informed approach fosters sustainable growth and encourages creators to experiment with new ideas while staying connected to their audience's interests.

10

Niche-Specific Content Ideas

RESEARCHING YOUR NICHE

Researching your niche is a critical step in revitalizing your YouTube channel. It involves understanding the specific interests, preferences, and behaviors of your target audience. Begin by analyzing the current trends within your niche. Utilize tools like Google Trends, YouTube search suggestions, and social media platforms to identify what content is gaining traction. These insights will help you pinpoint topics that resonate with viewers and can guide the development of your content strategy. By staying informed about emerging trends, you can position your channel to meet the evolving demands of your audience.

In addition to examining trends, competitor analysis is essential for understanding your niche landscape. Identify other channels within your niche and evaluate their content strategies, audience engagement techniques, and branding. Take note of what works well for them, such as their video styles, posting frequency, and community interaction. This analysis will not only inspire new content ideas but also reveal gaps in the market that your channel can fill. By differentiating your content from competitors, you can carve out a unique space that attracts and retains viewers.

Audience engagement techniques are crucial when researching your niche. Engage with your audience through polls, comments, and social media interactions to gather feedback on what they enjoy and what they would like to see in the future. This direct line of communication can provide valuable insights into their preferences and help you tailor your content accordingly. Additionally, consider segmenting your audience based on demographics or interests to create targeted content that speaks directly to each group. This approach fosters a deeper connection with your viewers and encourages loyalty to your channel.

Video SEO optimization is another vital aspect of researching your niche. Identify relevant keywords and phrases that your target audience is searching for. Incorporate these keywords into your video titles, descriptions, and tags to improve your visibility on search engines and YouTube. Tools like TubeBuddy and VidIQ can assist you in finding high-ranking keywords specific to your niche. By optimizing your content for search, you increase the likelihood of attracting new viewers who are interested in your niche, ultimately contributing to your channel's revival.

Lastly, consider leveraging social media for promotion as part of your niche research. Understand which platforms your audience frequents and how they consume content on those platforms. Each social media network has its own culture and style, so tailor your promotional strategies accordingly. Collaborate with other creators in your niche to expand your reach and tap into their audiences. Additionally, analyze your channel's analytics to track which promotional methods yield the best results. This data-driven approach will not only enhance your content strategy but also support the ongoing revitalization of your YouTube channel.

BRAINSTORMING UNIQUE VIDEO CONCEPTS

Brainstorming unique video concepts is essential for revitalizing a YouTube channel that may have stagnated. One effective approach is to tap into current trends and popular culture. By staying informed about what is trending on social media platforms, news outlets, and within the YouTube community, creators can identify timely topics that resonate with viewers. This not only ensures that the content is relevant but also increases the chances of attracting new subscribers who are searching for fresh perspectives on trending subjects. Incorporating these trends into your content strategy can breathe new life into your channel.

Another valuable technique is to engage directly with your existing audience. Utilizing polls, community posts, and comments can provide insights into what your viewers want to see. By asking for their input, you not only foster a sense of community but also generate unique ideas that are tailored to their preferences. Additionally, consider creating content that addresses frequently asked questions or common challenges faced by your audience. This not only positions you as a helpful resource but also encourages deeper engagement as viewers feel their needs are being acknowledged and met.

Exploring niche-specific content ideas can also set your channel apart. Many creators focus on broad topics, which creates competition and makes it harder to stand out. By diving deeper into specific sub-niches or combining different genres, you can carve out a unique identity for your channel. For instance, if your main focus is gaming, consider creating content that merges gaming with wellness or productivity tips. This approach not only broadens your potential audience but also showcases your creativity, making your content more intriguing and shareable.

Collaboration and networking can further enhance your brainstorming process. Partnering with other creators in your niche or even in complementary fields can lead to unique video ideas that you might not have considered alone. Joint projects can introduce your channel to new audiences and provide fresh perspectives on content creation. When brainstorming with collaborators, it's essential to focus on mutual interests and strengths, allowing for the organic development of concepts that appeal to both parties' audiences.

Lastly, leveraging analytics can inform your brainstorming efforts. Review your channel's performance data to identify which videos have resonated most with your audience. Look for patterns in viewer engagement, such as watch time, likes, and comments, to pinpoint what works and what doesn't. By understanding your audience's preferences through data, you can create more targeted and innovative video concepts. This approach not only revitalizes your content strategy but also ensures that your channel remains dynamic and responsive to viewer demands.

ADAPTING POPULAR TRENDS TO YOUR NICHE

Adapting popular trends to your niche can significantly enhance your YouTube channel's visibility and engagement. By identifying current trends in broader categories, you can strategically incorporate elements that resonate with your specific audience. Start by researching trending topics across social media platforms, news outlets, and popular YouTube channels. Pay attention to emerging trends in content formats, challenges, or themes that are gaining traction. The key is to find a balance between the trend's appeal and your unique content style, ensuring that your adaptations feel authentic and relevant to your viewers.

Once you've pinpointed a trend that aligns with your niche, consider how to tailor it to fit your audience's interests and preferences. For example, if you run a cooking channel and notice a trending recipe challenge on YouTube, you might adapt it by incorporating local ingredients or traditional cooking techniques that reflect your unique perspective. This not only keeps your content fresh but also establishes you as a creator who is aware of and engaged with the broader YouTube community while still remaining true to your niche. Crafting a narrative around the trend that speaks directly to your audience can boost engagement and foster a sense of community among your viewers.

In addition to content adaptation, consider the visual and branding elements associated with the trend. Analyze how successful creators are presenting their trend-related content. This includes examining their thumbnail designs, video titles, and overall aesthetics. By integrating similar visual strategies within your own brand guidelines, you can create a cohesive look that attracts new viewers while maintaining your channel's identity. Remember that consistency in branding enhances recognition, making your videos more appealing in a crowded marketplace.

Collaboration is another effective way to adapt popular trends within your niche. Partnering with other creators who are also tapped into the trend can amplify your reach and introduce your content to new audiences. When selecting collaborators, look for those whose content and values align with yours to create authentic partnerships. Joint videos, shout-outs, or even social media promotions can help both channels benefit from the trend, increasing engagement and potentially boosting subscriber numbers for both parties.

Finally, track the performance of your trend-adapted content through analytics to understand what resonates most with your audience. Pay attention to metrics such as watch time, audience retention, and engagement rates. This data will provide insight into how effectively you've adapted the trend and can inform your future content strategy. By continuously assessing and refining your approach based on audience feedback and performance data, you can create a dynamic channel that not only embraces trends but thrives on them, ultimately leading to a revitalized and engaged viewer base.

11

Monetization Strategies for Revived Channels

EXPLORING AD REVENUE OPTIONS

Exploring ad revenue options is a crucial aspect of revitalizing a YouTube channel. While many creators initially focus on content quality and audience engagement, understanding the intricacies of ad revenue can significantly enhance your channel's financial viability. YouTube's Partner Program allows creators to monetize their content through ads, but it is essential to grasp the various ad formats available. These include display ads, overlay ads, skippable video ads, and non-skippable video ads. Each format has its advantages and potential impact on viewer experience, and selecting the right mix can lead to increased revenue without alienating your audience.

To optimize ad revenue, creators must pay attention to their audience demographics, viewing habits, and peak engagement times. Analyzing your YouTube Analytics can provide insights into which videos attract the most viewers and generate higher watch time. This data is invaluable when deciding when to place ads in your videos. For example, if specific content consistently performs well, consider increasing ad placements during those videos or producing similar content to capitalize on viewer interest. Additionally, experimenting with ad formats and placements can yield different results, so continuous testing and adaptation are key.

Beyond traditional ad revenue, YouTubers can explore alternative monetization strategies that complement their ad income. Integrating affiliate marketing into your content allows you to earn commissions on products or services you recommend. This strategy can be particularly effective if you create niche-specific content, as your audience is likely to trust your recommendations. Furthermore, sponsorships and brand partnerships can provide significant financial support, especially if your channel aligns with a brand's target audience. Establishing a media kit that highlights your channel's reach, engagement metrics, and audience demographics can help attract potential sponsors.

Engaging with your audience not only builds loyalty but can also enhance your ad revenue potential. Building a community around your channel encourages viewers to return for more content, increasing overall watch time and ad impressions. Utilizing features like polls, Q&A sessions, and community posts can foster a deeper connection with your audience, making them more likely to engage with ads. Additionally, leveraging social media platforms to promote your videos can drive traffic to your channel, increasing views and subsequently, ad revenue. Regularly interacting with your audience across different platforms can create a cohesive brand presence that enhances your overall monetization strategy.

Finally, staying informed about changes in YouTube's monetization policies and ad revenue structures is essential for any creator looking to maximize their earnings. YouTube frequently updates its algorithms and community guidelines, which can directly impact ad revenue. Joining creator forums, attending workshops, or following industry news can keep you abreast of best practices and new opportunities. As you explore ad revenue options, remember that balancing monetization strategies with maintaining genuine content quality is vital for long-term success. By revitalizing your approach to ad revenue, you can ensure your channel not only survives but thrives in a competitive environment.

AFFILIATE MARKETING POTENTIAL

Affiliate marketing has emerged as a significant revenue stream for YouTubers and streamers, especially for those looking to revive their channels. By promoting products or services relevant to their content, creators can earn commissions on sales generated through their unique affiliate links. This not only offers a financial incentive but also enhances the value of the content they produce. For creators focused on revitalizing their channels, understanding the affiliate marketing landscape is crucial to harnessing its full potential.

One of the key advantages of affiliate marketing is its ability to integrate seamlessly into various types of content. Whether it's through product reviews, tutorials, or lifestyle vlogs, YouTubers can incorporate affiliate links without disrupting the viewer's experience. For instance, a tech reviewer can include links to the gadgets they discuss, while a beauty guru might promote cosmetic products used in their tutorials. This level of integration allows creators to maintain authenticity while monetizing their efforts effectively.

To maximize affiliate marketing success, it's essential to develop a content strategy that aligns with the chosen niche. Creators should select products or services that resonate with their audience and enhance their overall brand narrative. For those focused on reviving a stagnant channel, identifying relevant affiliate partnerships can reignite viewer interest and engagement. Collaborating with brands that share a similar audience can also lead to cross-promotion opportunities, expanding reach and boosting potential earnings.

Analytics play a vital role in optimizing affiliate marketing efforts. Creators should track which content drives the most traffic and conversions to their affiliate links. This data not only informs future content strategies but also helps in maintaining audience engagement. By analyzing viewer preferences and adjusting promotional strategies accordingly, YouTubers can create a more tailored experience that encourages viewers to act on their recommendations.

In conclusion, affiliate marketing presents a wealth of opportunities for YouTubers and streamers looking to breathe new life into their channels. By strategically integrating affiliate promotions into their content, creators can enhance viewer engagement while generating revenue. As they refine their content strategies, focus on analytics, and maintain authenticity, the potential for success in affiliate marketing will continue to grow, ultimately leading to a thriving channel.

CREATING AND SELLING MERCHANDISE

Creating and selling merchandise can be a powerful way to enhance your brand, engage your audience, and generate revenue for your YouTube channel. As a YouTuber or streamer, your merchandise should reflect your unique identity and resonate with your viewers. Start by brainstorming ideas that align with your content and audience preferences. Consider creating items like apparel, accessories, or digital products that incorporate your logo, catchphrases, or themes from your videos. This not only solidifies your brand identity but also gives your fans a tangible way to connect with you.

Once you have a concept for your merchandise, researching production options is crucial. You can choose to handle manufacturing and inventory yourself, which requires more upfront investment and commitment, or partner with print-on-demand services that handle printing, shipping, and inventory for you. These services allow you to focus more on content creation while still offering a variety of products. Whichever route you choose, ensure that the quality of your merchandise meets your brand standards, as this will affect your reputation and audience satisfaction.

Promoting your merchandise effectively is essential for driving sales. Utilize your existing platforms, such as your YouTube videos and social media channels, to showcase your products. Create engaging content around your merchandise, such as unboxing videos, behind-the-scenes looks at the design process, or styling tips. Collaborate with other creators or influencers in your niche to expand your reach. Consider running promotional campaigns, like limited-time offers or giveaways, to spark interest and encourage your audience to share your products with their networks.

Integrating merchandise into your content strategy can enhance viewer engagement. Mention your products during relevant videos and explain how they connect to your content or community. Encourage audience participation by asking for feedback on designs or product ideas. This not only makes your viewers feel involved but also provides valuable insights that can guide your future merchandise decisions. Incorporating merchandise in your videos can create additional touchpoints for audience interaction, fostering a stronger connection with your brand.

Finally, track your merchandise sales and analyze the data to understand what resonates with your audience. Utilize tools such as Google Analytics or e-commerce platforms' built-in analytics features to monitor performance. Pay attention to trends in sales, popular products, and customer feedback. This information can inform your future merchandise offerings and marketing strategies. By continually refining your approach based on data, you can ensure that your merchandise remains relevant and appealing to your audience, thereby sustaining your channel's revival and growth.

12

Consistency and Scheduling Plans

ESTABLISHING A POSTING SCHEDULE

Establishing a consistent posting schedule is crucial for revitalizing a dormant YouTube channel. A well-planned schedule not only helps maintain audience interest but also signals to the YouTube algorithm that your channel is active. This is particularly important for channels that have experienced a decline in engagement or viewership. By creating a predictable rhythm for your uploads, subscribers are more likely to turn on notifications and engage with your content regularly. The key is to find a frequency that aligns with your capacity to produce quality content while also keeping your audience engaged.

When determining your posting frequency, consider your niche and the type of content you produce. Some channels thrive on daily uploads, while others may perform better with weekly or bi-weekly postings. Analyze successful channels within your niche to gauge their posting habits and audience response. A trial-and-error approach can be effective; start with a schedule you feel comfortable maintaining, and adjust based on viewer engagement and feedback. Consistency is essential, but it should never come at the expense of quality.

In addition to setting a posting frequency, it's beneficial to establish specific days and times for uploads. Research indicates that certain days and times yield higher engagement rates, depending on your target audience. Utilizing YouTube Analytics can provide valuable insights into when your subscribers are most active. By aligning your posting schedule with these peak times, you can maximize visibility and engagement right after your content goes live. This strategic timing can significantly enhance your channel's revival efforts.

Promoting your videos across various social media platforms can also complement your posting schedule. By announcing upcoming videos and sharing teasers on platforms like Instagram, Twitter, or TikTok, you create anticipation and drive traffic to your channel. This cross-promotion can help you reach a wider audience and re-engage former subscribers. Ensure that your promotional content reflects your channel's branding and aesthetics, reinforcing the message and theme of your videos while encouraging followers to check out your latest uploads.

Finally, it's essential to remain flexible and responsive to your audience's needs. Regularly review your analytics to understand how your audience is responding to your posting schedule. If you notice a particular day or time results in significantly higher engagement, consider adjusting your future uploads accordingly. Engaging with your audience through comments or community posts can also provide insights into their preferences. By iterating on your schedule based on performance data and audience feedback, you can create a sustainable plan that revitalizes your channel and fosters long-term growth.

TIME MANAGEMENT TIPS FOR CREATORS

Time management is a critical skill for creators looking to breathe new life into their YouTube channels. Balancing content creation, audience engagement, and marketing efforts can be overwhelming, especially for those managing multiple platforms. To optimize your productivity, begin by establishing clear priorities. Identify your most important tasks, such as video production, audience interaction, and learning new SEO techniques. Create a to-do list that reflects these priorities, ensuring that you allocate your time effectively to the areas that will yield the greatest impact on your channel's revival.

Scheduling is another vital component of time management for creators. Develop a content calendar that outlines your video publishing schedule, social media promotions, and engagement activities. This not only helps you stay organized but also sets expectations for your audience. Regularly posting content fosters a sense of reliability and can significantly boost viewer retention and engagement. Utilize scheduling tools to automate social media posts, allowing you to focus on content creation while maintaining an active online presence.

Consider the Pomodoro Technique to enhance your focus and productivity. This method involves working in concentrated bursts, typically 25 minutes, followed by a short break. This structure can help creators maintain high levels of concentration while avoiding burnout. During these focused sessions, dedicate your efforts to specific tasks such as brainstorming niche-specific content ideas or optimizing video SEO. After each session, take time to reflect on your progress and adjust your strategies as needed.

Collaboration and networking are also essential for effective time management. Instead of working in isolation, reach out to fellow creators in your niche for joint projects or brainstorming sessions. Collaborations can streamline content creation processes and expose you to new audiences, ultimately saving time in the long run. Furthermore, sharing responsibilities, such as video editing or social media management, can allow you to focus on your strengths while benefiting from the skills of others.

Finally, regularly reviewing your analytics and performance metrics is crucial for refining your time management strategies. By analyzing which types of content resonate most with your audience, you can allocate more time to the creation of similar videos while minimizing effort on less effective formats. This data-driven approach allows creators to make informed decisions about their content strategy and engagement techniques, ensuring that every minute spent contributes to the overall revitalization of their YouTube channel.

STAYING MOTIVATED AND AVOIDING BURNOUT

Motivation is a crucial element for YouTubers and streamers striving to revive and maintain an engaging channel. The initial excitement of creating content can fade, leading to a feeling of stagnation. To combat this, it is essential to set clear, achievable goals that align with your overall vision for your channel. Break down larger objectives into smaller, manageable tasks, allowing you to celebrate small victories along the way. This approach not only helps maintain enthusiasm but also provides a sense of accomplishment that can propel you forward. Regularly revisiting these goals can keep you focused and remind you of the purpose behind your content.

In addition to goal setting, establishing a routine can significantly enhance your motivation. Create a content calendar that outlines your posting schedule, including deadlines for filming, editing, and promotion. This structure helps to create a rhythm that can reduce decision fatigue and increase productivity. Incorporating dedicated time for brainstorming and skill development within your routine will also keep your creative juices flowing. Engaging with your audience during this process, whether through polls or community posts, can provide valuable feedback and reinforce your connection with them, further fueling your motivation.

While striving for success, it is vital to recognize the signs of burnout. The relentless pressure to produce content can often lead to fatigue and a decline in creativity. Monitoring your mental and emotional well-being is critical. Ensure you are taking regular breaks and allowing time for self-care. Engaging in activities outside of content creation can provide fresh perspectives and rejuvenate your passion. Consider taking short breaks from your channel, using this time to recharge and come back with new ideas and energy. This deliberate pause can be a catalyst for renewed creativity and enthusiasm.

Collaboration can also play a key role in staying motivated and avoiding burnout. Partnering with fellow creators can introduce new ideas, perspectives, and audiences to your channel. This exchange not only alleviates some of the pressure of solo content creation but also fosters a sense of community and support. Regularly connecting with other YouTubers or streamers can inspire you to explore different niches and content strategies that you may not have considered. Building a network can lead to fruitful collaborations that can breathe new life into your channel and reignite your passion for creating content.

Finally, leveraging analytics can help maintain motivation by providing tangible evidence of your progress. Regularly review your performance metrics to understand what resonates with your audience. This data can guide your content strategy and help you make informed decisions about future videos. Celebrate the growth, no matter how small, and use it as motivation to continue evolving your channel. By remaining adaptable and responsive to both your audience's needs and your personal creativity, you can create a sustainable path that keeps you engaged and excited about your content while effectively avoiding burnout.

www.ingramcontent.com/pod-product-compliance
Lightning Source LLC
LaVergne TN
LVHW022229200926
848481LV00006B/2191
* 9 7 9 8 3 4 8 1 7 2 3 2 9 *